Australian
GEOGRAPHIC
BLUE MOUNTAINS

By Cathy Proctor

WOODSLANE PRESS

Woodslane Press Pty Ltd
10 Apollo Street
Warriewood, NSW 2102
Email: info@woodslane.com.au
Tel: 02 8445 2300 Website: www.woodslane.com.au

First published in Australia in 2019 by Woodslane Press in association with Australian Geographic
© 2019 Woodslane Press, photographs © Australian Geographic and others
(see acknowledgements on page 62)

NATIONAL LIBRARY OF AUSTRALIA

A catalogue record for this book is available from the National Library of Australia

Printed by KS Printers
Cover image: The Three Sisters, Katoomba by Chee-onn Leong | Dreamstime
Back cover: View to Mount Solitary from Prince Henry Cliff Walk by Showface - Dreamstime
Title page: Wollemi pine tree by Alessandrozocc/ Dreamstime
This page: An Australian native Eastern Spinebill feeding on nectar from a red Mountain Devil flower
Opposite: Govetts Leap sunrise
Book design by: Christine Schiedel
All other pic credits on page 62

CONTENTS

THE BLUE MOUNTAINS

With over 140 kilometres of walking trails and tracks that lead to spectacular scenery and breathtaking vistas, the Blue Mountains area attracts over 4 million visitors every year. Despite these numbers, the UNESCO World Heritage has listed the Blue Mountains as remaining relatively pristine: a 11,400 km² area of accessible wilderness, located just over an hour from Australia's largest city, Sydney.

Even from a distance, the Blue Mountains are instantly recognisable for their tell-tale blue haze, created when oil droplets from native eucalyptus trees mix with dust particles and water vapor in the air, causing certain wavelengths of light to reflect their intense blue color. But although they can appear blue, they are actually not mountains. The area is a series of uplifted plateau, dissected by canyons formed by a number of rivers carving through the sandstone bedrock.

Roughly 10 times older than the Grand Canyon, the landscape of the Blue Mountains is at once timeless yet constantly changing with the seasons, the weather and even the time of day. You'll be amazed at the diversity of diversity of ecosystems, the abundance of plant life and wildlife, and just how ancient and untouched this unique landscape feels.

■ Left: Crossing Greaves Creek on the Grand Canyon walking track

BLUE MOUNTAINS

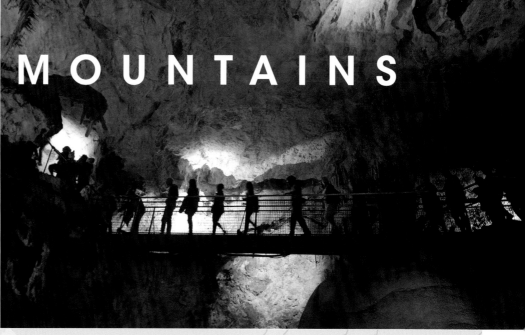

■ Right:
Exploring
Jenolan Caves

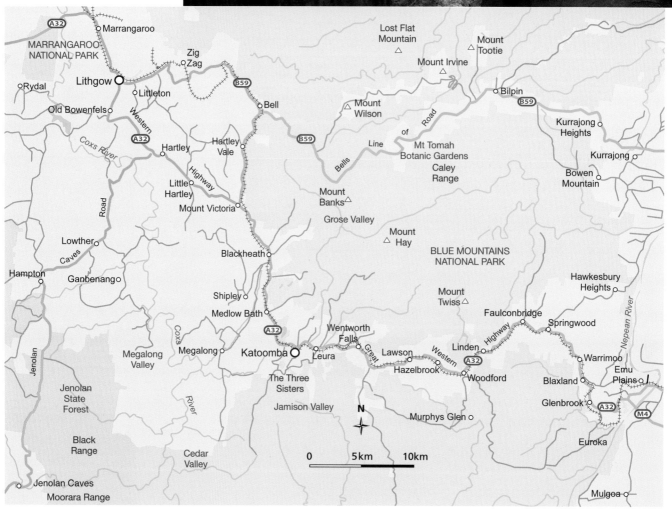

■ Above: Sylvia Falls is an impressive cascade of water in the gully of the Valley of the Waters at Wentworth Falls.

GEOLOGY

Characterised by beautiful 'mountains', deep canyons, ancient forests and spectacular sandstone plateaus, the Blue Mountains are part of the Great Dividing Range, which was formed around 50 million years ago. However, its geological history actually extends back to around 300 million years ago when the entire area was covered by an inland sea.

Large amounts of sediment were deposited into this sea from both inland, land-based glaciers, rivers and lakes as well as marine sources, and the subsequent sedimentation of these deep layers of sand, mud and coarse pebbles can still be seen today seen in the sandstone rock exposed along many of the of the Blue Mountains cliffs and escarpments.

Once these inland sea levels began to drop, river water and wind began to mould these rocks before volcanic activity caused a forceful uplift, raising the area upwards in a monoclinal fold. This formed the Great Dividing Range and the Blue Mountains plateau, which peaks at an elevation of around 1000 metres at Mount Victoria. Volcanic activity in the area also covered large areas of the mountains in basalt, which has mostly been worn away today but can still be seen in occasional outcrops on the high peaks.

■ Right: Jutting out over the Grose Valley, Hanging Rock near Baltzer Lookout, Blackheath is a huge, overhanging block of sandstone over 100 metres high.

CLIMATE

The cool and temperate climate of the upper Blue Mountains is enjoyed by both locals and tourists alike who relish the opportunity to experience its four distinct seasons. However, although the Blue Mountains has a reputation for snow, there are actually only around 5 snow days per year. The rainfall is similar to Sydney with the Upper Mountains receiving an average of around 1050 mm per year and the Lower Mountains around 850 mm per year. It's during these wetter months (November - March) that you're most likely to encounter mist and fog.

If you're lucky you might witness the "Phantom Falls", a rare but spectacular weather phenomenon caused by this mist and fog that occurs only once or twice a year, predominantly in Autumn and Spring.

Narrow Neck is a peninsula south of Katoomba and the meeting point of the Jamison Valley to the east and Megalong to the west. On a clear, still morning after rain when it's quite humid and fog sits low in both valleys, the rising sun first warms the air in the Jamison Valley, lowering the air density on that side. The differences in temperature and air pressure suck fog from the Megalong Valley across the top of Narrow Neck and into the Jamison Valley, giving the appearance of a ghostly, slow moving waterfall which is called the Phantom Falls.

Regardless of the time of year you visit the Blue Mountains, be aware that weather conditions can very quickly change, so always carry extra layers of clothing, sunscreen and water, especially when bushwalking and camping.

Above: Kangaroos in the snow.

Right: Eucalyptus forest on a foggy Blue Mountains day.

SUMMER

■ (December - February)
During the summer months it can occasionally get quite hot, but warm balmy days with cool summer nights are more the norm with temperatures ranging from 12-25°C.

AUTUMN

■ (March - May)
Temperatures range from 7-19 °C and these crisp mornings and cool nights are when the gardens are at their glorious best, especially in the historic villages of Mount Wilson and Mount Irvine.

WINTER

■ (June – August),
Winter is the peak tourist season with Christmas in July and Yulefest celebrations providing a taste of a Northern Hemisphere Christmas. It's a wonderful time for walking but you'll need to be well prepared if camping as temperatures range from 3-12°C, often dropping below zero at night, and frosts are common.

SPRING

■ (September to November)
As the temperatures start to rise in spring (7-19°C), visitors flock to the Leura Garden Festival and the Blackheath Rhododendron Festival to see the vibrant displays of trees, shrubs and flowers that thrive in this cooler climate.

PEOPLE

For tens of thousands of years and long before the European explorers and early convict settlers arrived in Australia, Aboriginal people have called the Blue Mountains home. The Gundungurra and Darug Tribes were the major indigenous tribes to inhabit the Blue Mountains, with the Burra Burra tribe inhabiting the nearby Jenolan Caves.

Aboriginal people still live in the Blue Mountains and there are plenty of opportunities for visitors to learn more about this ancient culture at the Blue Mountains Waradah Aboriginal Centre, the botanic garden at Mount Tomah, the rock art that adorns the walls of many rocks in the region, and the extremely well-preserved rock carving now known as "the flight of the Great Grey Kangaroo", which can be found near Hawkesbury Lookout. European's exploration of the region was delayed by the rough terrain until 1813, when explorers Blaxland, Wentworth, and Lawson formed an exploration group to search for accessible land, eventually opening up the Central West of New South Wales. The following year, William Cox and a team of convicts built a road in just 6 months across the mountains and all the way to Bathurst, where the Gold Rush in the 1850s brought an influx of Chinese and other travellers to the area and the eventual establishment of the railway line in 1867.

Today the 77,000 people who call the Blue Mountains home reflect the changing history of this place, including descendants of the original Aboriginal inhabitants, residents with European, German and Tibetan ethnicity, as well as Sydneysiders who settle here to enjoy exploring the natural beauty of the area, artistic community, affordable housing, historic architecture and cooler climate.

Above: The images in Red Hands Cave near Glenbrook are thought to have been painted between 500 and 1600 years ago. The cave showcases one of the best examples of Aboriginal art in the Blue Mountains.

Right: Most visitors to the Blue Mountains rarely venture far from the popular lookouts such as Echo Point. Those that do venture further discover some of the best bushwalking in Australia.

Below: The Road Builders Monument in Lilianfels Park, Katoomba, captures the interaction between indigienous and Eurpoean people in the early 1800s and pays respect to convicts who were used to build Cox's Road.

ECONOMY

The Blue Mountains Local Government Area covers 11,400 square kilometres of land, with about seventy percent of the total land area lying within the Blue Mountains World Heritage National Park.

There are just under 80,000 residents who live in the Blue Mountains but an additional 4 million people visit the Blue Mountains annually, with tourism generating over $400m per year. The region's Gross Regional Product is estimated at $2.51 billion, with healthcare, tourism, education and retail the largest employers in the area. In addition to the major tourist attractions there are many holiday homes and a lot of guest accommodation in the upper mountain towns, with industrial estates located in Katoomba and Lawson and a rural farming area in the Megalong Valley.

The Blue Mountains has a vibrant creative arts scene and was named Australia's inaugural 'City of the Arts' in 1998 - the only city to boast this moniker within a world heritage area. Many writers and artists are attracted to this creative hub, which hosts an annual Winter Magic Festival and Blue Mountains Writers' Festival, run by Varuna, the Writers Centre in Katoomba.

Visitors enjoy browsing the local shops and farmers markets that sell a selection of handicrafts, eclectic antiques, local produce and gourmet foods.

Above: The historic Jenolan Caves Guesthouse was built in 1897.

Left: Tourists enjoying the magical view of the Three Sisters from Queen Elizabeth Lookout, Echo Point, Katoomba.

Above: A koala hugs a Eucalypt tree while her joey hugs her back. Koalas are a marsupial native to Australia who live in Eucalypt trees with Eucalyptus leaves making up most of their diet. Joeys stay with their mothers for about a year, living six months inside her pouch and then six months outside. Unfortunately habitat destruction means they are now an endangered species in many areas.

Right: The Grey-headed flying fox is one of the largest bats in the world. This megabat is native to Australia with an average weight of up to a kilogram.

Far right: Unlike other native cockatoos, gang-gang cockatoos nest in hollow trees and this species is adversely affected by land clearing across south-eastern Australia. Gang-gang Cockatoos almost always use their left foot to hold food when eating.

C overing over 11,000 square kilometres, the Greater Blue Mountains World Heritage Area is one of the largest intact tracts of protected bushland in Australia and is home than 400 fauna species. Many rare and endangered species find refuge here in the lush rainforests, waterfalls, swamps and native eucalypt forests. The Blue Mountains not only contain some of Australia's most recognisable creatures (such as koalas, kangaroos and wallabies) but also many introduced species.

Over 130 species of birds live here, including native diurnal birds, four types of owl and 16 varieties of bat. In fact, the beautiful calls of bellbirds and whip birds will often be heard as you descend into the forests and gullies. But don't be fooled by the Superb Lyrebird - one of the world's largest songbirds, it is renowned for its excellent mimicry of other birds.

Most of the threatened species who live in the Blue Mountains are birds and bats, including the gang-gang cockatoo, glossy black cockatoo, powerful owl, masked owl, sooty owl, grey-headed flying fox, eastern bent wing-bat and greater broad-nosed bat.

Other elusive and rare animals to look out for include the Blue Mountains skink, the spotted-tailed quoll, the tiger quoll, long-nosed bandicoots, platypus (especially in the Grose River), yellow-bellied gliders, long-nosed potoroos, giant burrowing frogs, stuttering frogs, red-crowned toadlets and broad-headed snakes.

■ Below: A male superb fairy-wren sits on a tree branch near Jenolan Caves. Recognisable by their sky blue-coloured caps, which become iridescent during breeding season, new research has revealed that male fairy-wrens sing to their eggs and their chicks come out recognising their parent's unique song.

PLANTLIFE

The Greater Blue Mountains UNESCO World Heritage Area is one of the largest and most intact tracts of protected bushland in Australia, covered by a vast mantle of eucalypt forests, woodlands and mallee shrublands, along with smaller areas of rainforests, heaths, wetlands and exposed rock. It was added to the World Heritage List in 2000 in recognition of its significant natural values, including the rare and endangered plants that live here, such as the Wollemi Pine.

Bushwalking in the Blue Mountains gives you the opportunity to see firsthand many native plants, including over 90 different species of the magnificent eucalypt trees that give the mountains their blue colour, as well as rainforest plants, such as ferns. Some of the native flowers you'll see while bushwalking include Flannel Flowers, Bottlebrush, Gravillias, Waratahs (the state flower of NSW) and the Mountain Devil, which is the unofficial floral emblem of the Blue Mountains.

The Blue Mountains Botanical Garden at Mount Tomah showcases both native and introduced cool-climate species for which the region is also renowned. Visitors flock to Mt Tomah and the nearby community of Mt Wilson on Bells Line of road to witness the annual displays of spring flowers and blazing autumnal colours.

As well as the incredible private gardens that are open to the public as part of the Australian Open Gardens scheme, Mount Wilson is also the location of the Cathedral of Ferns Circuit and the Waterfalls Walk, both of which showcase the lush local rainforest environment.

Annual plant and garden festivals are held in Leura, Blackheath and Mount Tomah. The Campbell Rhododendron Gardens are also worth a visit during Blackheath's Annual Rhododendron Festival in November to see the beautiful mass plantings of rhododendrons and azaleas in bloom as well as during autumn when the deciduous trees are at their most spectacular. The Leura Gardens Festival is held in October when a variety of historic homes and gardens open their doors to the public, while the Wild About Waratah Festival is held every September at the Mount Tomah Botanic Gardens.

Opposite page: The many deciduous trees in the town of Mount Wilson makes for spectacular autumnal displays.

Far left: A waratah at Mt Tomah Botanic Gardens.

Left: The shape and felt-like texture of flannel flowers make this one of Australia's most iconic wildflowers.

Below: Cyathea dealbata, also known as the silver tree-fern, grows in the rainforest of Jamison Valley.

Previous page: Situated in Grose Valley, the Blue Gum Forest is a protected nature reserve that was saved from the axe by bushwalkers in the 1930s, who pooled their resources to purchase the land, preserving the forest for future generations.

Wentworth Falls is not only a town in the Blue Mountains, it is also the name of its most impressive and highest waterfall. This three-tiered, almost 200 metre-high waterfall cascades into Jamison Valley and can been seen from various lookout points.

Govetts Leap is another extremely tall and spectacular waterfall in the Blue Mountains region, falling 180 metres in a single drop into the Grose Valley. Named after William Govett, the first European settler to visit this area, the word "leap" means waterfall in old Scottish dialect. Govetts Leap is one of two waterfalls in the Blue Mountains that are also known as Bridal Veil Falls, because of their similarity to a long bridal veil. The other waterfall commonly referred to as Bridal Veil Falls is the Leura Falls, located in the Jamison Valley.

The Jamison Valley is also home to the most photographed waterfall in the Blue Mountains, the Katoomba Falls, which is a 150 metre-high staircased waterfall, situated between Echo Point and Scenic World. But if you're after a quieter waterfall experience, away from the crowds, a short but very steep walking track starting at the Conservation Hut in Wentworth Falls will reward you with not one, but three waterfalls: the Empress Falls, the Sylvia Falls and the Lodore Falls.

Very experienced and extremely fit hikers can take in the delights of the Silver Cascades and Victoria Falls, both located in the Upper Blue Mountains along the Grose River. But if you're less abled and short on time, a much more easily accessed but equally rewarding waterfall is the Leura Cascades. This small stacked waterfall is nestled quietly between shrubs and ferns in the heart of the valley and accessed via a short but scenic walk that leads to a shaded picnic area, ideal for families.

Above: Katoomba Falls proximity to the Three Sisters makes it a must-see spot.

Right: Looking up at Wentworth Falls, easily the Blue Mountains' most famous and dramatic falls.

Following page: Leura Cascades is a popular picnic area set amidst tall eucalypts.

CANYONS

LOWER BLUE MOUNTAINS

Often bypassed by tourists for the more famous attractions of the Upper Blue Mountains, the historic towns and natural attractions of the lower Blue Mountains have their own special charms and are usually far less crowded. The climate is also a lot warmer than in the higher towns, making it an ideal destination for a winter's walk or a swim in summer.

In Glenbrook the banks and shallow areas of Jellybean Pool and its large sandbank make it an ideal swimming spot for children. Its quieter and usually more secluded neighbour, Blue Pool, is only a short walk away, offering idyllic swimming in a deeper and longer fern fringed pool, all within a tranquil bush setting.

Glenbrook not only has a thriving café culture but it also is the access point to Euroka Campground, thought by many to be Sydney's best bush camping experience. When you camp at this idyllic and secluded bush campsite, surrounded by tall gumtrees, kangaroos are sure to visit. Child friendly bush walks nearby include the Euroka Creek Trail and the easy circuit Link Track, which will bring you to one of the best Aboriginal stencil galleries in the Sydney Basin, the Red Hands Cave.

As you head up the mountains, the National Trust listed Norman Lindsay Gallery and Museum at Faulconbridge is well worth a visit for art lovers, as well as history and architecture buffs.

Lawson has one of the very few walking tracks in the Blue Mountains where dogs are more than welcome. The 3-kilometre long South Lawson Waterfall Circuit Walk includes an off-leash dog park located at an old golf course within the track. You'll get to experience four very different waterfalls along this track: Adelina Falls, Junction Falls, Federal Falls and Cataract Falls.

Top left: Jelly Bean Pool.

Opposite page bottom: Euroka: extremely popular with both campers and wildlife.

Left: Norman Lindsay House.

WENTWORTH FALLS

The historic town of Wentworth Falls lies at the centre of the Blue Mountains and offers some of its most spectacular and accessible bush walks and views. This charming town was originally named 'Weatherboard' and then 'Jamison's Valley' before finally being changed to Wentworth Falls in 1867 in honour of explorer William Charles Wentworth. Wentworth Falls picnic area is the starting point for several family friendly tracks, such as the Charles Darwin trail that will take you along Jamison Creek. The more challenging Overcliff-Undercliff track combines scenic clifftops, birdwatching, and rainforest with waterfalls including the magnificent Empress Falls in the picturesque Valley of the Waters, which is one of the prettiest spots in the Blue Mountains.

The National Pass is one of the Blue Mountains' classic walks, with its epic lookouts over the Jamison Valley and the historic hand carved Grand Stairway, but at the time of going to print this walk was temporarily closed between Valley of Waters and Slacks Stairs due to a rockfall, so check with National Parks and Wildlife before attempting this walk.

Many bushwalks in the Wentworth Falls area have incredible lookouts that offer breathtaking views, such as Breakfast Point Lookout, Princes Rock Lookout and Rocket Point Lookout. The Wentworth Falls Track takes you on a level path past Jamison and Wentworth lookouts before descending to the spectacular Fletchers lookout, while the Wentworth Pass trail includes the Queen Victoria Lookout, Empress Lookout and the Lyrebird Lookout.

Cafés and restaurants around this beautiful area include the Grandview Hotel, which was built in 1924, the historic Conservation Hut Conservation Hut at the Valley of the Waters, which has been a valued rest stop for hikers for many years, and the not to be missed traditional German bakery and coffee shop, Patisserie Schwarz.

■ Previous page: Easterly views of Glenbrook Creek before it enters the Nepean River.

Right: Wentworth Falls. After heavy rain, lots of water from Jamison Creek drops over the escarpment and plunges about 180 metres into a large pool before flowing down the Valley of the Waters.

Opposite page: Sunset and sunflare on the grand stairway in the cliffs of the National Pass, which was built in the early 1900s along the cliff ledge. A a zig zag stairway down the sheer cliffs to the mid-level falls gives many visitors pause for thought.

Left: A misty day on the National Pass, one of the Mountains' favourite walks (when it's not closed by rock falls!).

Below: A wooden path section on the Charles Darwin walk.

THREE SISTERS AND

Standing at nearly 1000 metres above sea level, the Three Sisters at Echo Point, Katoomba, is the Blue Mountains' most popular landmark, visited by millions of people every year. According to Aboriginal legend, this iconic rock formation represents three sisters who were turned to stone by a witchdoctor to protect them from harm. There are a wonderful range of walks that begin at Echo Point, including the family-friendly Three Sisters Walk, affording you stunning views of the Three Sisters, the Jamison Valley, the Ruined Castle and Mount Solitary from the cliff top. The Prince Henry Cliff walk takes you past many scenic lookouts along the cliff edge on your way to Leura Cascades, but if you'd prefer to descend into the Jamison Valley below, the Three Sisters Walk will take you to Scenic World and Katoomba Falls via the incredible Giant Stairway, which consists of over 800 steel and stone steps.

Along Cliff Drive you will be spoilt for choice with a number of lookouts, including Eaglehawk Lookout, Landslide Lookout, Cahills Lookout, Narrow Neck lookout, Cliff View Lookout, Wollomai Lookout, Allambie Lookout and Lady Darly Lookout. The town centre of Katoomba features historic art deco buildings, vintage clothing shops, cafes and antique shops. The Edge Cinema screens a fascinating Blue Mountains wilderness documentary on its giant screen, taking you to places in the Blue Mountains which you may never be able to discover yourself.

The first hotel to be built in Katoomba in 1882 was The Carrington Hotel, which still attracts visitors to the area today with its heritage architecture and annual Yulefest celebrations. Other major Katoomba Festivals include the Six Foot Track Marathon in March and the Winter Magic Festival in June.

KATOOMBA

Previous page: The classic view in the Blue Mountains.

Above: For those willing to stretch their legs the Honeymoon Bridge will get them up close and personal with one of the sisters.

Left: Katoomba Falls

SCENIC WORLD

Scenic World is one of the most popular tourist attractions in the Blue Mountains thanks to the incredible breathtaking views of the Three Sisters, Katoomba Falls and Jamison Valley offered via its skyway, cableway, railway and walkway.

Over 25 million passengers have ridden the Scenic Railway since its inception in 1945 and an award-winning redevelopment in 2013 provides expansive views of the rainforest setting and spectacular Jamison Valley through the glass-roofed carriages.

The steepest passenger railway in the world (with a 128° incline) descends 310 metres through a cliff-side tunnel to the Jamison Valley floor where you can either return to the top of the cliff in your railway carriage or meander through the ancient rainforest of the Jamison Valley floor via the Scenic Walkway.

The walkway is 2.4 kilometres of elevated boardwalk, with plenty of rest benches, exploring elements of the site's coal mining history while immersing you in the Jurassic rainforest. If you visit during May you'll enjoy the outdoor sculpture exhibition, Sculpture at Scenic World. Both the fully-enclosed and wheelchair accessible Scenic Cableway and the glass floored Scenic Skyway provide incredible aerial views of the Three Sisters, Orphan Rock, Mt Solitary, Katoomba Falls and the Jamison Valley. The Scenic Cableway gently descends into the Jamison Valley, allowing you to access the Scenic Walkway, whereas the Scenic Skyway glides between clifftops.

Opposite page: The steepest passenger railway in the world, the Scenic Railway is a funicular railway which uses a cable traction to move the glass-roofed railway carriages up and down the steep inclined slope.

Top left: Bronze sculpture of a miner and his pit pony on the Scenic Walkway.

Left: Scenic Skyway in mist.

Bottom: The Scenic Cableway is the steepest and largest aerial cable car in the Southern Hemisphere, descending 545 metres into the Jamison Valley.

Previous page: Breathtaking views of the Three Sisters and Jamison Valley from the Scenic Skyway.

GROSE VALLEY

Much of the Grose Valley has been preserved as wilderness, thanks to its bottleneck shape and the steep escarpment walls that lie on either side of this spectacular landscape of chasms, canyons and cliffs, ensuring only walkers can access its natural beauty. Its wide upper area includes the Blue Gum Forest before narrowing into the Kolonga Canyon and then finally emerging on to the plains at Yarramundi where the Grose River joins the Nepean River.

On the northern side of the valley, the main access point is via Pierces Pass (also known as Hungerford Track), off Bells Line of Road. However, the major tracks into the valley are accessed at Blackheath in the Upper Grose Valley. Perrys Lookdown is the most popular entry point into the Grose Valley, also providing a direct route to the magnificent Blue Gum Forest, which is a spectacular protected nature reserve. A more challenging walk commences from Govetts Leap lookout, where you can take in scenic waterfall views during your steep descent.

Evans Lookout is the starting point for the Grand Canyon walking track, an awe-inspiring 3-hour hike that will take you through a variety of canyons and eco-systems, while enjoying spectacular valley views, creek crossings, some decent descent and ascents, temperate rainforest sections and numerous waterfalls, including the remote Beauchamp Falls.

Previous page: View from Pulpit Rock of the majestic Grose Valley.

Opposite page: Moon rise over Yarramundi, where the Grose River narrows before flowing into the Nepean/Hawkesbury River system.

Left: The walk through the Grand Canyon would be a strong contender for 'Best Walk in the Blue Mountains' and one of the best in Australia.

Beyond the crowds of Katoomba's Three Sisters and Scenic Skyway, the other Upper Blue Mountains towns of Leura, Medlow Bath, Blackheath and Mount Victoria offer a quieter Blue Mountains experience, along with the possibility of snow in winter thanks to their higher altitude.

Leura attracts many day trippers and shoppers with its excellent selection of cafés, restaurants, boutiques and homewares that line Leura Mall. But outside of the main shopping area you'll also find some of the most classic and beautiful walks and waterfalls in the Blue Mountains, including the Leura Cascades Walk, the Federal Pass and the Prince Henry Cliff Walk. Everglades, the 5.2-hectare Paul Sorensen designed European garden, also affords extraordinary views of the Australian wilderness.

The glamorous art deco surrounds of the recently restored Hydro Majestic Hotel in Medlow Bath is a great spot to take in the stunning views of the Megalong Valley. Even more spectacular vistas are to be found at Blackheath viewpoints, including Evans Lookout, which is the starting point for the clifftop walk to Govetts Leap and Pulpit Rock, with its three levels of lookouts affording an almost 360° view. The Fairfax Track is family friendly and wheelchair accessible along the entire length of this clifftop walk.

There are two historic theatres in the upper Blue Mountains. The old Victory Theatre in Blackheath is now the largest antiques centre west of Sydney and it also operates a bustling café, but the Mount Vic Flicks, located in heritage-listed Mount Victoria, is still operating as a working cinema.

Mount Victoria is the most western village of the Blue Mountains and gateway to the delightful towns that dot Bells Line of Road, including the apple orchards of Bilpin. From Mount Victoria you can also explore forests and caves of Fairy Bower or head west into Kembla Grange, Little Hartley and Lithgow.

Above: The Victory Antique Centre in Black-heath.

Left: Pulpit Rock lookout is becoming increasingly popular as people discover this out-of-the-way but astonishing vantage point.

MEGALONG VALLEY

The Megalong Valley, the Jamison Valley and the Grose Valley are the three major valleys in the Blue Mountains, however the Megalong is the only one of these three valleys that you can drive into with a two wheel drive vehicle and experience firsthand the lush ferns and rainforest which cover the escarpment.

The Hydro Majestic Hotel at Medlow Bath provides breathtaking views across the Megalong but access to the valley is further up the Blue Mountains at Blackheath, where you turn off the Great Western Highway at the railway crossing and then follow the signs to descend into the valley. This quiet and peaceful valley was home to the Gundungurra Aboriginal people for 40,000 years before Europeans arrived and the word Megalong is a Gundungurra Aboriginal word meaning 'valley under the rock', a reference to its location below Narrow Neck.

Today the Megalong Valley is primarily a farming community, with many visitors making the trip down to eat at the historic Megalong Tea Rooms or enjoy some of the best horse-riding adventures available in Australia.

Walkers on the famous Six Foot Track descend via the temperate rainforest of Nellies Glen to the Megalong Valley, where the track winds along the steep-sided banks of the Coxs River.

■ Left: Few visitors venture this far into the Blue Mountains, making it all the more wonderful for those that do.

Right: Kangaroos love the Megalong!

Below: An old cart outside a riding school in Megalong Valley.

Opposite page: It's easy to believe you've slipped back a few decades when visiting this picturesque area.

THE SIX FOOT TRACK

I n 1884 a New South Wales government party was sent to survey a route for a horse track to connect Katoomba to Jenolan Caves. The track had to be at least six feet wide to allow two loaded drays to pass each other at any point. After years of construction, the first recorded passage of the completed track was by the governor of the day, Lord Carrington, in September 1887.

The Six Foot Track was maintained for many years by two men using a wheelbarrow, picks and shovels, but by the 1930s it had became impassable due to lack of maintenance. It was reopened in 1984, following reconstruction work, as a 45-kilometre walking trail through the World Heritage listed national park. Today the exhilarating and challenging route is enjoyed by both bush walkers and runners alike, with hundreds of entrants participating in the annual Six Foot Marathon race which follows the length of the entire trail.

The track, a challenging 2 or 3-day hike, gives you the opportunity to experience heritage sites, heath, woodlands and rainforest, with several excellent overnight campsites at Old Ford Reserve, Coxs River, Black Range and Alum Creek. You can walk the track in either direction but if you start on the western outskirts of Katoomba at the Explorers Tree, you'll descend steeply through the temperate rainforest of Nellies Glen to the Megalong Valley floor. The track then winds along the steep-sided banks of the Coxs River, where you'll cross the river using the Bowtells Swing Bridge before climbing the range and finally, arriving at Jenolan Caves.

This historic track is best walked in the more temperate seasons of spring or autumn and if you're unable to complete the entire walk, shorter sections can also be undertaken.

■ Right: Views across to Norths Lookout and Nellies Glen and the start of the Six Foot Track.

Right: Coxes River, from under the bridge.

Below: Carlotta Arch is a large and spectacular cave remnant, located at the Jenolan Caves' end of the six foot track.

Opposite page: Bowtell Suspension Bridge.

THE JENOLAN CAVES

Located in the Blue Mountains World Heritage Area, 175 kilometres west of Sydney and 30 kilometres west of Katoomba, the Jenolan Caves is arguably Australia's most spectacular, possibly largest and certainly most visited cave system. The caves were created about 340 million years ago, through a complex relationship between water, rock, atmosphere and the lifeforms that inhabit the environment, making them one of the oldest cave systems on Earth.

The local Aboriginal people called these caves Binnomea, which means dark places, and since European settlers discovered them in the 1830s, more than 40 kilometres of multi-level passageways have been explored and mapped.

Daily tours (including weekend night tours) are conducted in 11 of the caves in this stunning network of ancient limestone tunnels, subterranean rivers and caverns, with coloured lights defining and enhancing the most spectacular stalactites and stalagmite formations. Tours are available for all ages and levels of fitness. Highlights include the enormous Cathedral Chamber (more than 50 metres high) in the Lucas Cave, the "ribbon" helictites of the Ribbon Cave, the Angel's Wing (a 9-metre shawl formation in the Temple of Baal Cave), and the Minaret, Grand Column, Queen's Canopy and River Styx in the River Cave, which is the most demanding of the cave tours.

Accommodation is available onsite at the historic Jenolan Caves House, from where you can also explore the local area (including the stunning Blue Lake) via a variety bushwalking tracks.

Previous page: Amazing limestone stalagmite and stalactite formations in the Orient Cave, considered by many to be the most beautiful cave in the Jenolan caves.

Opposite page: The 'Minaret' is an enormous and spectacular stalagmite located in the Tower Chamber, the first main chamber of the River Cave.

Top: The stunning blue water of the 'Pool of Reflections', part of the underground 'River Styx' that runs through the River Cave. This deep, illuminated underground lake has an almost motionless surface that produces mirror-perfect reflections.

Above: The natural colouring of the Blue Lake at Jenolan Caves is a side effect of the minerals the water picks up passing through the caves. Patient observers can sometimes see platypuses swimming in this lake.

Sitting at 1,016 metres above sea level, the village of Mount Tomah is located on the Bells Line of Road and can be accessed via either the townships of Richmond or Mount Victoria. The village is most famous as the location of the Blue Mountains Botanic Garden, 28 hectares of curated garden and a further 244 hectares of wilderness that sits inside the UNESCO World Heritage Area. With its rich and fertile volcanic soils, Mount Tomah is a showcase of both local and imported cool climate plants and alpine rainforest.

Gardens include the Formal Garden with its traditional European garden design and the Rock Garden, featuring rocky plant communities from different continents. But don't miss the Bog Garden, a hanging swamp with carnivorous plants where you will find kneeling pads so you can get close to the Venus' Fly Trap, sphagnum moss and other rarities that grow in the cool, moist climate of the Blue Mountains region.

Other highlights include conifers and cultivars such as the rare Wollemi Pine, giant Redwoods, rhododendrons, Brown Barrel Eucalypts, the Blue Mountains Basalt Cap Forest and the North American Woodland, which comes to life with rich, warm colours in Autumn.

Previous page: The stunning autumn colour of Mount Tomah Botanical Gardens.

Opposite page: A kookaburra patiently looking for his next meal.

Left: One of the many kilometres of paths that wind in and around the gardens.

ACKNOWLEDGEMENTS

Cathy would like to thank all the talented photographers whose work is included here. She would also like to thank Andrew Swaffer for his enthusiasm and commissioning the series; Christine Schiedel for her design skill and patience; and Jenny Cowan for the map, And finally, love and thanks to her family: Peter, Samuel, Benjamin and Superman, the crazy German Shorthair Pointer.

ABOUT THE AUTHOR

Cathy Proctor is the author of many travel and health books, including The Caravan & Campervan Cookbook, Sydney for Dogs (now in its 4th edition), and Sydney's Best Beaches & Rock Baths.

Her lifelong love affair with the Blue Mountains began as a young child on family holidays, before moving to Lithgow as teenager gave her even more opportunities to explore and get to know the area. When not researching and writing books, Cathy writes websites and runs her own cooking school.

ABOUT THE PUBLISHERS

The Australian Geographic journal is a geographical magazine founded in 1986. It mainly covers stories about Australia - its geography, culture, wildlife and people - and six editions are published every year. Australian Geographic also publish a number of books every year on similar subjects for both children and adults. A portion of the profits goes to the Australian Geographic Society which supports scientific research as well as environmental conservation, community projects and Australian adventurers. www.australiangeographic.com.au.

Woodslane Press are a book publishing company based in Sydney, Australia. They are the publishers of Australia's best-selling walking guides and under their co-owned Boiling Billy imprint also publish camping, bush exploration and 4WD guides. For more than a decade committed to publishing books that empower Australians to better explore and understand their own country, Woodslane Press is proud to be working with Australian Geographic to produce this new series of souvenir books. www.woodslane.com.au.

Also available from Woodslane Press:

All images are protected by copyright and have been reproduced with permission.